# The Chick on the Thick Brick

**Pam Scheunemann**

Consulting Editor, Diane Craig, M.A./Reading Specialist

ABDO
Publishing Company

Published by ABDO Publishing Company, 4940 Viking Drive, Edina, Minnesota 55435.

Printed in the United States.

Credits
Edited by: Pam Price
Curriculum Coordinator: Nancy Tuminelly
Cover and Interior Design and Production: Mighty Media
Photo and Illustration Credits: AbleStock, Tracy Kompelien, Photodisc

Library of Congress Cataloging-in-Publication Data

Scheunemann, Pam, 1955-
    The chick on the thick brick / Pam Scheunemann.
        p. cm. -- (First rhymes)
    Includes index.
    ISBN 1-59679-461-5 (hardcover)
    ISBN 1-59679-462-3 (paperback)
        1. English language--Rhyme--Juvenile literature. I. Title. II. Series.

PE1517.S3599 2006
808.1--dc22

                                                                    2005048049

SandCastle™ books are created by a professional team of educators, reading specialists, and content developers around five essential components that include phonemic awareness, phonics, vocabulary, text comprehension, and fluency. All books are written, reviewed, and leveled for guided reading and early intervention reading, and designed for use in shared, guided, and independent reading and writing activities to support a balanced approach to literacy instruction.

# Let Us Know

After reading the book, SandCastle would like you to tell us your stories about reading. What is your favorite page? Was there something hard that you needed help with? Share the ups and downs of learning to read. We want to hear from you! To get posted on the ABDO Publishing Company Web site, send us e-mail at:

**sandcastle@abdopub.com**

**SandCastle Level: Beginning**

## -ick

**brick**

**chick**

**kick**

**stick**

**tick**

This is a .

Here is a .

He is doing a .

This is a .

See the 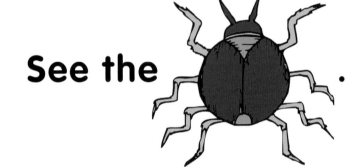 .

# The brick is red.

# This chick is yellow.

# Tim likes to kick.

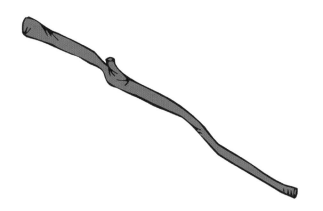

# The stick is long.

A tick is a bug.

# The Chick on the Thick Brick

Up on the hill,
there is a thick brick.

On the thick brick
sits a yellow chick
named Rick.

Rick the chick
has a friend
who is a tick.

The tick visits Rick
at the thick brick.

Rick the chick
says to the tick,
"Hop on that stick
to get on top of
the thick brick!"

Then Rick the chick
jumps on the stick
with a quick kick.

Now the tick
is on top of
the thick brick
with Rick the chick!

# About SandCastle™

A professional team of educators, reading specialists, and content developers created the SandCastle™ series to support young readers as they develop reading skills and strategies and increase their general knowledge. The SandCastle™ series has four levels that correspond to early literacy development in young children. The levels are provided to help teachers and parents select the appropriate books for young readers.

**Emerging Readers**
(no flags)

**Beginning Readers**
(1 flag)

**Transitional Readers**
(2 flags)

**Fluent Readers**
(3 flags)

These levels are meant only as a guide. All levels are subject to change.

To see a complete list of SandCastle™ books and other nonfiction titles from ABDO Publishing Company, visit **www.abdopub.com** or contact us at:
4940 Viking Drive, Edina, Minnesota 55435 • 1-800-800-1312 • fax: 1-952-831-1632